IMAGES
of America

FORT KENT

It has been said that U.S. Highway 1 "begins with pines and ends with palms." The journey, consisting of 2,446 miles of highway spanning 14 states and the District of Columbia, begins at Fort Kent in the north and ends at Key West, Florida. In 1948, this signboard was posted by the Fort Kent Chamber of Commerce on the outskirts of town. The town itself was named from a block house that was built in 1939, when a boundary dispute almost brought armed conflict between the United States and Canada.

On the cover: This photograph was taken in June 1900 by area photographer Michele Morin of Portage Lake. Morin was in town to photograph the graduating class at the Madawaska Training School. While in town, he also photographed school buildings and this panoramic view of the village. (Courtesy of Leroy Martin.)

IMAGES
of America

FORT KENT

Laurel J. Daigle

ARCADIA
PUBLISHING

Published by Arcadia Publishing
Charleston SC, Chicago IL, Portsmouth NH, San Francisco CA

Library of Congress Control Number: 2008937073

For all general information contact Arcadia Publishing at:
Telephone 843-853-2070
Fax 843-853-0044
E-mail sales@arcadiapublishing.com
For customer service and orders:
Toll-Free 1-888-313-2665

Visit us on the Internet at www.arcadiapublishing.com

*The book is dedicated to Rose Nadeau Sinclair, a lifelong resident
of Fort Kent who has always had interest in the community.
Over the years, Rose has been an advocate of the town
and sought to promote it in every way.*

CONTENTS

ACKNOWLEDGMENTS

The author is indebted to a number of individuals and organizations that offered encouragement and assistance. Heartfelt appreciation goes to the individuals that lived part of this history and provided the author with historic information and photographs. Lise Pelletier Soucy and Ann Chamberland from the Acadian Archives of the University of Maine at Fort Kent were always helpful in locating and sharing early photographs from their collection. Annette Daigle, president of the Fort Kent Historical Society, and Anna Raymond willingly made available the resources of the society. Chad Pelletier, a local history enthusiast, shared his fine collection of early Fort Kent photographs. My wife, Priscilla, offered her support and editorial assistance in the process of putting the book together. Finally Hilary Zusman from Arcadia Publishing was always able to answer my questions, and her assistance was invaluable.

INTRODUCTION

An early-20th-century account of Fort Kent describes it as a "picturesque village located in the upper St. John River Valley," where the waters of the Fish River unite with those of the St. John. It was predicted that the town's scenic attraction and favorable climate would make it a resort of the future. Early settlers that came here around 1829 were predominantly French-speaking Acadians. The Acadians were refugees driven to this northern wilderness to escape the oppression of the English. By oral tradition, José Nadeau has commonly been known as the first settler of Fort Kent. At the time of settlement, a census report found Nadeau in Ste. Hilaire, New Brunswick, and not in Fort Kent. We know with certainty, however, that Nadeau and his family were among the early settlers, and the family places prominently in early political, economic and religious life of the community.

The area quickly became known for its vast lumber resources, and individuals with an entrepreneurial spirit were quick to develop business interests in the region. A dispute arose as both the United States and the British government made claim to the land. As a result, armies took a defensive posture to protect their claimed interest. The dispute never developed into a full military conflict, and the border issue was settled in 1842 by the Webster-Ashburton Treaty. Settlement of this issue meant that the people could more fully concentrate on agriculture and lumbering pursuits. Mills that produced finished wood product were established, and the rivers were used to bring the lumber to markets elsewhere. As the town became more organized, common schools were established to educate the population although teachers were in short supply. To remedy the situation, Maj. William Dickey, who represented the area in the Maine legislature, was successful in acquiring funds to establish a teaching training school in Fort Kent. The institution, known as the Madawaska Training School, was the precursor of what is now the University of Maine at Fort Kent.

An economic boom occurred when the railroad came to town in 1902. It provided passenger services and a means of transporting goods and services to the outside markets. Subsequently the area became less remote and more easily accessible.

The Catholic religion, faith of the Acadians, also recognized the needs of the people. In the early 1900s, Fr. Arthur Decary, a Catholic priest, was successful in acquiring the services of the Little Franciscan Sisters of Mary to staff St. Louis School, a church initiated school in Fort Kent. At the urging of another priest, the sisters later established and operated a hospital that is currently the Northern Maine Medical Center. The sisters made a significant contribution to the life of the community until they withdrew from Fort Kent in 1999.

The town has had a history of perpetual spring flooding that usually occurs with the melting of a heavy snowfall that coincides with spring rains. Fort Kent received some relief in the 1970s when the federal government funded a dike project that has since protected the West Main Street area from floods.

Over the years, Fort Kent has developed into a thriving cosmopolitan service community for the upper St. John River valley. Of service to the area are a modern medical center and a University of Maine campus. Tourists are offered an opportunity to experience life without the heavy traffic and bustle of a fast-paced urban life. Outdoor recreational opportunities thrive during all four seasons of the year. Families with roots in the area often return here to retire.

One

FORT KENT'S PAST

This photograph from 1900 was taken where the Fish River empties into the St. John River. Because the town was situated at the river juncture, it was earlier known as La Grande Décharge. In earlier times, the town was also referred to as the "Fish River settlement." At one point, Fort Kent was part of a larger area in the upper St. John Valley known as Hancock Plantation. The area was regarded as a remote point on the northern frontier, where the pioneering families chose to settle. Early on, the rivers provided settlers with their only means of transportation. (Courtesy of Bill Pinkham.)

The early French settlers were generally impoverished and had little formal education. As a group, they were industrious and hard workers. Some even became great improvisers and skilled craftsmen. They capitalized on the area's natural resources and engaged in agricultural and lumbering pursuits. They were people that did not seek a lavish lifestyle but yearned for a simple life close to the earth surrounded by one's children. The Great Depression was a time of extraordinary hardships.

These photographs were taken by Jack Delano in October 1940. Delano worked for the Farm Security Administration (FSA), traveling throughout the United States photographing farming enterprises that were clients of FSA. Places photographed in Fort Kent portrayed the pervasive poverty that plagued the area during these early hard times. (Courtesy of FSA Collection, Library of Congress.)

José Nadeau, sometimes called Joseph Nadeau, has always been thought of as the patriarch of Fort Kent. Living memories of people, referred to as oral history, is the basis for creating this story. This kind of history is understandably difficult to verify. It can be said with confidence that Nadeau was among the first settlers, having arrived in 1829. At the time, he was about 20 years old. He first married Seraphine Martin at St. Basile in 1833, and they had six children, all girls. When his first wife died, José married Alice White in 1848, and six children resulted from this union, Joseph, Richard, John A., Henry W., Alice E., and Cynthia.

The Dube House, now owned by the Fort Kent Historical Society, was built in 1840 on the banks of the St. John River. It is one of the oldest houses in Fort Kent. In 1865, the house was relocated to the corner of Dube Street and Route 1. Recently donated to the society, the house had been in the Dube family for four generations.

This is an image of the Dube family taken in their home in December 1906. Seen here are, from left to right, (first row) Ernest and Felix; (second row) Alice with baby Yvonne Laferriere, Adolphe Jr. (Threasa's father), and Adolphe Sr.; (third row) Phylias Laferriere, Agnese Dube, and Willie Lamarre. Willie may have been a boarder at the home.

Farming was the principal occupation in Fort Kent. Clearing and cultivation of fertile flats along the river was the primary focus during the first decades of settlement. By the late 1830s, the premier *rangs* of Acadian farmers were well established and prepared to supply the needs of the people. Pictured above is an 1895 photograph of oxen and a horse pulling hay wagons on West Main Street. In the background is the Cunliffe building that later became known as the Masonic lodge.

In 1930, John Desjardin could rightly be proud of his potato crop. His claim was partly due to the fertilizer he was using and promoting. Desjardin's farm was situated on the Sly Brook Road in Fort Kent. Desjardin was typical of the many small farmers that grew potatoes as their main crop.

A flourishing lumber industry soon developed, providing an economic alternative to sons who may not have inherited land from their parents and who otherwise would have left the area to earn a livelihood. Because winter was the most favorable season for working in the woods, an alternative pattern of farming and lumbering was developed. At that time lumber was "king" and massive pines were in demand. Some of the lumber entrepreneurs also engaged in the business of retailing and hostelries. The photograph above, taken in the early 1950s, shows, from left to right. Gerard Plourde, and brothers Valerie and Lucien Jandreau harvesting pulpwood with their horse team.

The Masonic lodge building was built in 1892 by William H. Cunliffe Sr. However, Freemasonry in Fort Kent dates back to the mid-1800s, though only formally organized at the beginning of the 20th century. In 1904, the masons in Fort Kent rented the top floor of the Cunliffe building for $125 a year. They later purchased the building. For years, this corner of Main Street has been referred to as the "Mason Block." To this day, the Masonic lodge in Fort Kent continues to be an active community organization.

In the 1930s, the school conveyance for students was pulled by horses. It consisted of an enclosed rectangular box on a sleigh. It was equipped with a wood stove to keep the students warm as they made their way to school. The photograph was taken in front of the Ligouri Robichaud house on East Main Street.

The 1919 Fort Kent Athletic Association basketball team was rightly proud of their record. They played teams across the state of Maine. Home games were played at Woodman Hall where the Century Theater is now located. Identified here are, from left to right, (first row) Jim Hoyt and Joe Berry; (second row) Bill Burgoyne and ? Levesque; (third row) Andrew Michaud, Joe Klein, and Albenie Long.

In 1939, Fort Kent had a semi-professional baseball team that was the champion of the Aroostook League as well as district champions of the National Semi-Pro Baseball Congress. Seen here are, from left to right, (first row) Wilfred Sappier, Bob Ruth, Mason Goodrich, Harvard Whitten, John Whitten, and Romeo Marquis; (second row) manager and coach James "Pop" Hoyt, Oneil Doucett, Red Clark, W. Murray, L. Blier, and Bert Daigle.

Fort Kent has always been a patriotic community. During World War II, Fort Kent citizens expressed their community spirit by participating in metal salvage drives to help the war effort. The salvaged material was hauled and deposited near the railroad tracks in Fort Kent where they could be readily loaded on the train. In this early 1940s photograph is a view of Highland Avenue beyond the salvaged material.

These early 1900s photographs are of the building complex that was the Madawaska Training School. To the far right is Cyr Hall named after Vetal Cyr, its first principal. Money was appropriated for the building in 1889. Cyr Hall provided the school with classrooms, a general assembly room, and library.

The building at right was Nowland Hall, a boarding house that was built in 1891. Within a few years, an ell was built to accommodate increased enrollment. Part of the Model School is seen on the right.

In 1891–1892, four Bradbury brothers and John Mullen came to Fort Kent from New Limerick and purchased mill property and a store on the Fish River. Their business was named the Fort Kent Mill Company. In 1895, John Mullen sold his interest and the firm continued as a corporation with Mrs. Lester Bradbury as chief owner. Niles C. Pinkham was president and Grover C. Bradbury was secretary-treasurer. The mill became known as the leading industrial establishment in the Fort Kent area.

The plant had a rotary mill, seven shingle mills, and a clapboard and lathe machine. The company was cutting an average of 20 to 25 million shingles and more than a million feet of long lumber annually. The firm also operated a gristmill and a carding mill. In the roller mill, they could ground as much as 53,000 bushels of buckwheat in a single season. A dam on the river, with a head of 14 feet, provided power to operate the mill.

The mill's office and general store carried a complete line of general merchandise and lumbermen's supplies. The company shipped large quantities of hay and grain. It also dealt with fertilizer, farm and garden seed, farm implements, carriages, sleighs, harnesses, and horse equipment. The mill employed teams comprising of 120 to 140 men in their lumbering operation.

The company owned a 350-acre farm cultivating 150 acres of it. The farm produced 1,400 barrels of potatoes, 110 tons of hay, and 1,200 bushels of grain. In 1919, the mill was sold to the Great Northern Paper Company who never operated the mill. In 1926, the International Paper Company acquired ownership. The buildings were eventually torn down. The store was rented by Thomas Pinkham Sr., who operated it for another 29 years.

This 1901 photograph shows the construction of abutments when a railroad bridge was built to cross the Fish River above Fort Kent Mills. The photograph above shows the completed bridge that was ready for the line to open in December 1902. With the arrival of the railroad in 1902, there was noted increase in the production of potatoes in Fort Kent. Some 600 carloads of potatoes were shipped from Fort Kent in the "big year" of 1906.

The Bangor and Aroostook (B&A) also carried large amounts of hay, grain, shingles, and pulpwood. Fort Kent was also a shipping point for the sportsman that came here to hunt. During 1907, 19 deer and 4 moose were shipped in the first mouth of the open season. Business at the Fort Kent Post Office doubled during the first years of the B&A's operation, according to F. W. Mallett, postmaster in the early 1900s.

R. R. Station, Ft. Kent, Me.

The train station is the town's most significant and intact building associated with the community's early-20th-century economic development. Opened on December 15, 1902, the station served the area until 1979 when it was retired. It was originally the northern terminus of the Fish River Railroad when it commenced operation over 51 miles of track from Ashland to Fort Kent. The Bangor and Aroostook Railroad was able to add Fort Kent as its northern point when it acquired the railroad on July 8, 1903. The above photograph was taken in 1910.

VIEW OF FORT KENT. MAINE-

Fort Kent received a good deal of attention in the promotional literature of the B&A. It claimed, "in all Maine no railroad scenery surpasses that along the Fish River division of the B. & A. Railroad between Eagle Lake and Fort Kent." The station initially consisted of a baggage room, general waiting room, women's waiting room, and offices for the station agent and road master. The arrival of the train to the town depot was the highlight of the day. People came to see the "going ons" and to socialize with the passengers. Everything came by rail, even the Barnum and Bailey Circus.

When retired in 1979, the train station was deeded to the Fort Kent Historical Society, which maintains it as railroad museum. Over the years, the station received improvements, such as a shingled roof and repairs to the foundation. This 1980 photograph shows the station as seen by the viewing public today. It is the most northerly railroad station in New England. It houses a museum of early historic artifacts related to railroading. The society's plan is to preserve and promote it as a living part of Fort Kent's heritage.

Thibodeau Insurance Agency was founded in 1902 by Paul D. Thibodeau. At the time the photograph was taken in August 1940, the business was at a West Main Street location, in a building commonly known as the Thibodeau Block. In the photograph are, from left to right, Loretta (Pelletier) Thibodeau, and Paul's sons, Omer, Romeo, and Philip. In 1978, the business relocated to East Main Street in Fort Kent.

This is a look inside a store that was owned by M. J. Pelletier during the early 1940s. In 1944 the store became Daigle and Daigle after it was sold to David D. Daigle and Gerald Daigle. In 1945, the store burned but was rebuilt.

The building was originally built at the time of the Bloodless Aroostook War to house soldiers and was known as the "Barracks." It was later used as a residence by Maj. William Dickey and his son Cyrus H. Dickey. Mary Page Allen of Bangor and Washington, D.C., daughter of Margaret Dickey and A. G. Fenlason, had the distinction of being the only child born in the Barracks. It became a hotel in 1901.

Hotel Dickey was one of the best-known hostelries in northern Maine until it was destroyed by fire on May 25, 1928. One reporter visiting Hotel Dickey in 1908 noted that proprietor "McInerney sets an excellent table and the cuisine would appease the appetite of the most fastidious." At that time, the main hotel had 22 rooms with an extra 9 rooms "outside."

The Military Square was situated in the vicinity of where the town library is today. It was a center of commerce with the George H. Page Store and Warehouses, H. W. Sawyer Jewelry Store, and the Swift and Company office. H. W. Sawyer had a well-equipped jewelry establishment and dealt in postcards and photographic souvenirs.

The George H. Page Store carried a complete stock of groceries, dry and fancy goods, shoes and lumbermen's supplies. He was also a large purchaser of hay for shipment and dealt in grain and mill feed, fertilizer, farming tools, lime, and cement.

The G. H. Page Residence, FORT KENT, Me.

The stately home of George H. Page was in the area now occupied by the Paradis Mall. Its architectural beauty was unsurpassed by any other building in Fort Kent. According to Irenee Cyr, he and others helped build the mansion in 1895. Its architectural style was that of an English Victorian design with shingles forming an ornamented pattern. It had a cone-topped turret that made it particularly attractive. Much to the chagrin of some Fort Kenters, the building was torn down in the late 1960s to make way for the mall complex.

A town landmark was the Fort Kent Hotel that was situated in front of the present Rite-Aid store on East Main Street. It was owned by Jos. C. Levesque of Clair, New Brunswick. It was destroyed by fire in December 1913. After the fire, two small buildings, believed to be owned by the Cannan family, were built on the same lot. The buildings were rented by Alfred D. Soucy in 1924 when he started his grocery store and farm supply operation.

The Arcadia, pictured in these 1939 photographs, was owned by Peter Toschi and was another Fort Kent establishment that catered to the traveling public. Situated where Bee-Jay Tavern is currently located, it was destroyed by fire in 1945.

At the beginning of the 20th century, Hotel Morneault was another fine hotel in Fort Kent. It was situated in the area later occupied by the Sol Cote Jewelry Store on West Main Street. The hotel was destroyed by fire on January 2, 1933. In front of the hotel are bikers ready for a race.

The Audibert Store was owned by Stephen Audibert. Audibert was married to José Nadeau's youngest daughter, Cynthia. Audubert did a brisk business selling sporting goods and general hardware.

In 1920, Philippe A. Roy saw a need for a general store in Fort Kent. He built on the corner of Market and Main Streets. It was constructed of red brick and had two stories with a full cellar. The upstairs became the Roys' living quarters, with rooms for boarders. The general store sold items such as matches, nails, saws, animal feed, and groceries. Next to the general store was a farm equipment store owned by P. Valier Roy, a son of Philippe. There was a stable next to the store for horses. When customers shopped, they had a place to rest and feed their horses. Both the general store and the farm equipment store did a good business. The corner of Market and Main Streets was more than a busy intersection; it was then the hub of the town. To make money on weekends, young boys would stand on the street corner with their shoe-shine boxes.

This postcard photograph is of the Fish River Bridge looking east. The steel bridge was constructed by the American Bridge Company in 1908. On the far right is what was then St. Louis School and is now an apartment complex. The postcard was postmarked June 17, 1952, with the message "this is the bridge that Erland is working on. We like it here. It's a nice town and everyone is so nice."

On West Main Street, where Nadeau's House of Furniture is now located, was the Chypias Nadeau store that sold home furnishings. As a service community for the area, Fort Kent merchants served a large clientele.

BANK BUILDING & CUSTOM HOUSE, Fort Kent, Main
Published by S. Burrill, Fort Kent, Maine

Among some early financial institutions was the Fort Kent Trust Company. The Fort Kent Trust Company commenced business in 1903 and was situated in a central location in the village. It was initially organized by John A. Nadeau, son of José Nadeau. Its board was later headed by Cyrus H. Dickey. In 1908, it had a capital stock of $50,000 and undivided profits of $2,916.09, with deposits aggregating to $120,448.90. Unfortunately the bank fell victim to the Great Depression. Its investors, who were largely from the area, experienced significant financial losses. The bank office was later used as a town office. The 1905 photograph shows the location of the bank building on upper West Main Street.

Lower Main St., Ft. Kent. Me.,
Showing Post Office,
Bank and Custom House.

This 1906 postcard shows a number of early-20th-century businesses in Fort Kent. To the left of the road and in the forefront was the Henry Nadeau store. Henry Nadeau was the son of Jose and the grandfather of Omer Thibodeau. On the same side of the street was the Frank Mallett building with the Fort Kent Telephone Company office building attached to it. Also visible are the cables that held the footbridge over the St. John River. On the right side of the street was the Fort Kent Trust Company. Also part of the trust company was the customs house as the bank's president was the collector of customs.

Another early financial institution in Fort Kent was the First National Bank that was located in the Thibodeau Block on West Main Street. It was organized in 1919 with Paul D. Thibodeau as its first president. The bank weathered the Great Depression and continued to serve the area well into the 20th century.

The George T. Quigley Hardware Store, located on the north side of West Main Street, is pictured here as it was in 1960. In 1974, a new structure was built to the rear of this building. The old store was then torn down to make way for a parking lot. The small building on the right was the office used by William B. Pinkham, a woods operator.

In Fort Kent, the slogan "one stop shop" rightly applied to the Jake Etscovitz enterprises. Etscovitz was a contractor and speculator in potatoes, second-hand cars, new cars, bicycles, radios, vacuum sweepers, and "hot" and classical music. This photograph shows him at his business in 1942. (Courtesy of Library of Congress Collection, John Collier Photographer.)

In this 1940 photograph is the Etscovitz Sons Garage, a business that started in 1929. In 1969, owner Harry Etscovitz was employing 45 people and looked forward to a bright future. (Courtesy of Library of Congress Collection.)

Farmers were often unable to afford new vehicles, so Jake always carried a good supply of secondhands available. The Etscovitzs were one of the few Jewish families in town. Son Harry gave his mostly Catholic employees holy days off as paid holidays.

An all-voluntary Fort Kent Fire Department was formally organized in 1919 with Joe H. Nadeau as fire chief and Sol Cote as assistant fire chief. The town eventually supported the department with the purchase of a fire truck in 1923. Nadeau remained fire chief until his death in 1963. The following volunteers were part of the department in 1936. From left to right are Arthur Audibert, Rosaire Lizotte, Nadeau, Jim "Pop" Hoyt, Edward Doyle, Sol Cote, Paul Soucy, and Rex Dow. On the truck is Theodore Charette.

Three ferries and a suspended footbridge connected Fort Kent with the Canadian town of Clair on the opposite side of the St. John River. The suspended bridge was constructed by Joseph Long Sr. in 1903 and was about 720 feet in length. The footbridge was especially useful in the fall and spring months when the river was dangerous to cross because of high water and floating ice.

Foot Bridge in winter, FORT KENT, Maine.

Pedestrians that used the suspension bridge paid a 5¢ toll that was later increased to 10¢. During prohibition, some people from Fort Kent would cross over the bridge to enjoy an alcoholic beverage. Depending upon how much alcohol consumed, some complained that the suspension bridge swayed on their return to Fort Kent.

FORT KENT, MAINE ST. FERRY

The connection to the Canadian side of the St. John River was important to Fort Kent as relatives were commonly found on both sides of the river.

The J. B. Levesque ferry allowed vehicle passage between the two towns of Fort Kent, Maine, and Clair, New Brunswick. It operated until the International Bridge was completed in 1930.

In 1929–1930, the International Bridge was built in Fort Kent, and there was no longer a need for ferry crossings and the suspension bridge. While Maj. William Dickey had worked tirelessly for the bridge, he died before it became a reality. Advocating for its construction was left to others, such as Dora Pinkham, who represented the town in the legislature at the time of the bridge construction.

INTERNATIONAL BRIDGE, FORT KENT, MAINE   1597

In 1940, farmers and their trucks waited outside the Starch Plant for hours for their potatoes to be graded and weighed. The plant was owned and operated by George H. Page. It was located on the Fish River. Tons of low-grade and small potatoes were processed at the plant each year. (Courtesy of Library of Congress Collection.)

This photograph is of the factory in the 1940s. In an average season, the output of this factory was about 130 tons of starch. When high prices prevailed for potatoes or when there were fewer small and low-grade potatoes, the output was only about 32 tons. Starch factories went by the wayside when wastewater could no longer be discharged in the river.

The Daigle brothers, Alcide and Irenee, farmed adjoining river lots on the Frenchville Road. As was the custom, parents lived their entire life in a family setting. "Grandpa" Hilaire Daigle lived his last days with his son Irenee. Marie Albert lived with her daughter and son-in-law, Gertrude and Alcide H. Daigle. This was at a time when there were no community-based services for the elderly. This 1944 photograph is of Hilaire Daigle, a grandchild, and Marie Albert.

River lots, such as lot number 41 on the Frenchville Road, were particularly valued because of the fertile soil along the river valley. The photographs picture the picking of potatoes in 1949 on the Alcide H. Daigle farm. For identification purposes, the farmer's initials were painted on the barrels. The hand pickers placed potatoes in baskets that were emptied into barrels.

The barrels full of potatoes were mechanically hoisted on the bed of a truck and transported to a storage barn. When emptied, the barrels were returned to the field to be filled with potatoes again.

Mechanical harvesting eventually replaced most of the hand picking of potatoes. Because of safety issues, working on a harvesting is limited to older, high school–age students. Fort Kent schools close for two weeks so that students can help out with the harvest. This 1975 photograph shows a mechanical harvester operation on the Thibeault flats near the Fort Kent/Frenchville town line.

For years, Fort Kent was promoted as a sportsmen's paradise. Early B&A brochures carried many articles about the region as a way to increase rail traffic to the area. The 1930s postcard was taken at the Jalbert Sporting Camps in the Allagash.

The Jalberts were registered guides with a great love of the outdoors. They were also civic-minded and placed prominently in the early life of the community. The barn with the bear-skin "trophies" was on St. John Road in the vicinity of what is now the golf course.

Over the years, the area has had record snowfalls that make travel particularly challenging. Some winter snows came in October and remained until early May. This photograph, taken on the Cross Lake Road in the 1930s, pictures Roland Page, a local attorney, in the midst of very high snow banks.

Fort Kent capitalized on its heavy snowfall by developing recreational activities. The first ski-tow in Fort Kent was a private initiative. It was owned and operated by the Philip Pelletier family on the Frenchville Road and called the "County Ski Tow." In recent years, Klein Hill was developed into a ski area that has also become popular in the winter. There are cross-country skill trails and snowmobile trails that are kept groomed and are enjoyed by many.

One of the highlights was Fort Kent's parades that usually occurred on Memorial Day and the Fourth of July. It was a time for the town to showcase its fire trucks, as seen in this photograph of the 1940s. The photograph was taken on West Main Street, showing the Daigle and Bouchard Hardware store and Ouellette's Clothing and shoe store in the background.

Rock Ouellette began a business while still in high school, setting up a small lunch counter in a downtown building. He entered the military in 1942, returning to Fort Kent in 1945 when he bought Jean-Louis Page's place to continue his business. In 1955, he moved his building to the site where the business is today. In 1957, he built a motel. Ouellette later sold his business to Mickey Levesque. In recent years, the business was purchased by Peter Pinette.

Fort Kent had the distinction of being the most northerly railroad station in New England. During World War II, soldiers left for war by passenger train. The station in Fort Kent was where relatives and loved ones gathered to bid their last farewell to the soldiers and other travelers.

This 1940 photograph is of the Fort Kent Drug Company that had a pharmacy and a soda fountain and carried merchandise typically found in drug stores. The store was a popular gathering place for area people who came to socialize over coffee. It was located on the south side of West Main Street where there is now the Radio Shack Store. (Courtesy of Library of Congress Collection.)

In earlier times, the town was operated by the selectmen who received a modest stipend for their work. As municipal management became more complex and demanding, town officials hired Elbridge Gagnon as the town's first full-time manager in 1945. Gagnon remained in this position for 23 years. Gagnon, pictured with his wife Sylvia in the early 1960s, had graduated from St. Mary's College in Van Buren and had been chairman of the board of selectmen in Frenchville from 1929 to 1938.

Succeeding Gagnon as town manager was Claude Dumond, Fort Kent's second town manager. It was during Dumond's tenure that a dike was built in 1977 to control flooding of the business district on West Main Street. In 1978, a new municipal center was constructed at a cost of $451,000. The old town office building was torn down to make way for the new customs building.

Under Dumond's guidance, the town celebrated its centennial with much gusto in 1969. To kick off the celebration, a centennial mass was celebrated by his Excellency Bishop Peter L. Gerety of the Diocese of Portland. The outdoor mass was attended by over 500 people with civic and religious organizations participating.

A huge parade of 50 entries was held on Sunday, June 29, 1969. It proved to be the biggest parade Fort Kent had ever seen. Parading down Main Street were bands, civic and religious groups, town police, and the fire department.

Over 27,000 spectators lined the parade route, cheering the participants on. This photograph shows an array of antique cars that were part of the parade.

Two

BORDER DISPUTE AND MILITARY OCCUPATION

BLOCK HOUSE, BUILT IN 1838, FORT KENT, ME.

The Fort Kent blockhouse is located at the confluence of the Fish and the St. John Rivers in Fort Kent. This state-owned structure is the only extant fortification relating to the Bloodless Aroostook War of 1839, and the border dispute between Great Britain and the United States. The first defender of the fort was a state militia that was later replaced by federal troops. The signing of the Webster-Ashburton Treaty of 1842 settled the boundary dispute between Maine and New Brunswick, and reduced the need for a fort, although federal troops remained in Fort Kent until 1845.

This is a 1930 photograph of Monument Square in Fort Kent that was used as a parade ground during the Aroostook War. It was a short distance from the blockhouse where the public library is now situated. A large building was erected for the barracks and two large double tenement houses for the accommodation of the officers. The other buildings consisted of a hospital, commissary store, stable, and blacksmith shop. The only building that remained standing for some time was Maj. William Dickey's residence in the vicinity of what was Robert Jalbert's home on Pleasant Street. After the raising of the colors in the morning, the men paraded in review of their commanding officer. At sunset, the troops reassembled at the parade ground for retreat, when the flag was lowered.

On the south side of the Monument Square was the old barrack building that later became the residence of Maj. William Dickey. Dickey had repaired and modernized the building. It was here that the first town meeting in Fort Kent was held on Saturday, April 3, 1869.

To have an effective military force in Fort Kent, all realized the need for accessibility through an improved roadway. Monies were appropriated to establish a road of about 46 miles from Masardis to the St. John River. The road was initially known as the Military Road and is now known as Route 11. Roadwork, under the charge of Col. Charles Jarvis of Ellsworth, commenced in September 1839 and continued through the winter. The wages paid the men was $18 per month for common laborers and a higher rate for special services. When the road was established, it was generally of poor quality and made for difficult passage.

The Block House in Fort Kent is the most photographed historic building in town. It was built of hewn timber 20 inches thick and on a high point of land. It was meant to protect a 400-foot boom that was strategically placed to stop timber cut by trespass lumbermen. In the midst of a diplomatic war with Great Britain and New Brunswick over the northern boundary of the state, Maine anchored its claim to the southern half of the St. John Valley with this fortification in 1839. It stood as the chief guardian of American and Maine interests while boundary negotiations dragged on in national capitals.

Subsequently the fort was abandoned and suffered neglect. A family in the 1850s took residence within it. In the early 1900s, someone took the initiative to cover the upper section of the building with clapboards to hide the holes made in the timbers for windows.

In the 1920s, the fort received a newly-shingled roof and the dormers were removed. In the 1950s, state monies were appropriated to repair the blockhouse and bring it to its original condition. All the original hewn pine timbers were retained in the original condition. Today the blockhouse is one of the finest tourist attractions in the northeast. During the summer months, local boy scouts are present as tour guides and tell its story.

Following the state militia's fortification of Fort Kent, Lucien Webster and his federal troops arrived here on September 17, 1841, in time to prepare for their first winter in the northern wilderness. In March 1842, Webster lamented that Fort Kent was "still buried in the depth of winter, the snow falling on us constantly." His life as a military officer was spent in Maine, Connecticut, Florida, and Texas. Webster was later promoted to lieutenant colonel. He died of yellow fever in Texas during a military campaign. (Courtesy of State Museum of Pennsylvania.)

Lucien's wife, Francis, some six months pregnant, had remained in Houlton but followed her husband to Fort Kent later that fall, giving birth to a daughter in November. She requested that an older, more experienced doctor attend to "her confinement" in Fort Kent. Francis complained that being the only lady at the post, she had "no female society." Social life was limited to officers of the garrison and occasional visits from British officers in the vicinity. Francis's happiness in Fort Kent was centered on her two little girls that gave her "abundant occupation," so much so "that I have little leisure to regret my isolated position." (Courtesy of Fort Sill Museum, Oklahoma; portrait by A. T. Haddock,)

In April 1844, federal troops were again sent to Fort Kent. Citizens, concerned with a lack of civil authority there, had petitioned for a continued army presence. Capt. John H. Winder and his Company G 1st Artillery unit arrived at this "northernmost possession of the army and the most desolate and isolated post in the East." Winder was shocked to find that drunkenness was a big problem at his new post and quickly banned alcohol. He felt that his mission could be jeopardized when "drunken soldiers inevitably get into fights with British civilians." Winder later resigned from the army to join the Confederacy, where he was promoted to brigadier general.

Three

FORT KENT SCHOOLS

Soon after the treaty of 1842, James C. Madigan came to Fort Kent to establish schools in the Madawaska territory. School sessions were sometimes shortened or interrupted because of seasonal demands of labor, such as potato harvesting. The Lincoln School was typical of the early rural schools in Fort Kent. It was located at the junction of Sly Brook and Caribou Roads. Pres. Franklin D. Roosevelt's New Deal provided each student with a free hot lunch. The photograph was taken in 1941. Fire destroyed the Lincoln School during the winter of 1943.

These students attended the Lincoln School in the spring of 1941. Seen here are, from left to right, (first row) Beulah Marin Madore, Harold O. Bouchard, Beulah Bouchard Dubois, Norman Nadeau, Laurette Bouchard Rioux, and Alva Bouley; (second row) Gilbert Bouley, Joel Bouchard, Edmund Bouchard Jr., Merril Bouchard, and Joan Bouchard Raymond; (third row) Gilman Dube, Joella Marin Charette, Delores Bouchard Leonard, Louis Jack Bouchard, Josephel Bouchard Jr., and Louis Morin; (fourth row) Leroy Dumond, Alban Bouchard, Louis Philip Lozier, Norman Morin, and Robert Nadeau.

The Reed School was another Fort Kent rural school that was in the Violette Settlement. It was one of the schools that closed after Market Street School was opened. Like many of the other rural schools, the Reed School had no electricity and only primitive toilet facilities. The photograph was taken in 1946.

This photograph is of students at Reed School during the 1945–1946 school year. The teacher is Gertrude I. Daigle.

From 1878 to 1920, the high school in Fort Kent was actually the Madawaska Training School. When the high school building was built in 1920, it consisted of grades 9 and 10, with the upper grades being at the Madawaska Training School. Increased high school enrollment required adding an additional unit to the building in 1948. It was also necessary to separate students into two groups, one in attendance in the morning and the other in the afternoon. The curriculum was broadened by building a shop building in 1950 and providing a course in industrial arts.

Seen here is the 1907 graduating class at Madawaska Training School. From left to right are (first row) Zeniade Audibert, Mary Ann Albert, Marie Labbe, Sophie Boutot, Mary Michaud, and Helen Lang; (second row) Flavie Cyr, Dina Plourde, Anastasia Daigle, Albertine Audibert, Lucie Cyr, Catherine Daigle, Marie Daigle, Elizabeth Daigle, Anna Guy, and Rose Nadeau; (third row) Arthur R. Daigle, Francois Hebert, Fred Morin, Felix Beaulieu, ? Brown (instructor), and Euphemia Roy; (fourth row) Thomas Pinkham, James Marquis, Eddie Cyr, and Thomas Dee.

As enrollment at the Madawaska Training School increased, the need for a boarding house became evident. Principal Vital Cyr lamented to the proper state authorities that some individuals could not enroll because of a lack of accommodations in the school's vicinity. A boarding facility for 50 to 60 students, later named Nowland Hall after the school's second principal, was constructed in 1891. Within a few years, an ell containing a classroom, recitation rooms, model schoolroom, and a large stairway was added to the building. Howland Hall was situated between the old Cyr Hall on the right and the Model School in the extreme left. The building was destroyed by fire in 1955.

The Model School, an elementary school associated with the Madawaska Training School was opened in September 1909. The rooms at the school were described as "battered, dark and cold." Two teachers were in charge of the school that consisted of two rooms that could each accommodate 40 pupils. In 1928, students in grades three and four at the Model School seen here are, from left to right, Wilfreda Toschi Ouellette, Margaret Larson, Joyce Ramsey, Lena Plesset, Angelina Bouchard, Dorothy Bradbury, Alma Coury, ? Pelletier, Bernice McCormack, Barbara Crocker Goodrich, Arnold Eaton, Edmund Bouchard, Kenneth Roberts, Guy Baker, Fred Roberts, Richard McLellan, and Lewis Plesset. The teacher is Marion Pinette.

Area teachers with minimal training attended summer school to complete requirements for certification. Attending the Madawaska Training School summer session in the late 1940s are, seen here from left to right, (first row) Leonard Sutherland, Ludger Michaud, Abel Morneault, Leroy Smith, Guy Baker, vice principal Floyd Powell, secretary Rinette Theriault, principal Richard F. Crocker, instructor Lillian Michaud, Patricia Paradis, Anita Plourde, Louise Drake, Anita Ouellette, instructor Yvonne Garceau, and Theresa Young; (second row) Edna Daigle, Bernadette Gagnier, Pauline Scott, Laurette Tardie, Bertha Dube, Donaldine Cyr, Muriel Tardif, Lucille Levasseur, Albina Marquis, Alfreda Fournier, Jean Demers, Viola Tardif, Alice Labrie, Ann Crocker, Amelia Daigle, Theresa Dumond, Mamie Michaud, and Celina Cyr;

(third row) Sister Patrick, Sister Dominique, Josephine Gagnon, Sister Rachel, Sister of the Annunciation Adeline Jandreau, Rowena Dumond, Blanche Michaud, Yvonne Long, Mabel Vallancourt, instructor Waneta Blake, Marietta Martin, Bernice Labbe, Essie Bouchard, Hilda Dumont, Sister Priscille, Sister Alphonse, Sister des Lys, Sister Benvenu, instructor Dorothy Bryant, and Juliette Michaud; (fourth row) Sister Rita, June Roy, Cecile Nicknair, Bertha Demers, Mary Picard, Alice Labbe, Rita Labrie, Sister Theresa, Sister Octave, Sister Amboise, Pearl Pelletier, Fern Pelletier, Pearl Morrison, Sister John, Gladys Gardner, Sister Jacqueline, Sister Ermine, and Alice Young.

GYMNASIUM MADAWASKA TRAINING SCHOOL, FORT KENT, ME. 415.

The Madawaska Training School's gymnasium was constructed in 1928. According to principal Richard Crocker, it permitted the addition of physical education to the curriculum. The building is now the Blake Library, named after Wanita Blake, an early teacher and librarian at the school.

This is a 1916 photograph of Dickey Hall, named after the man who contributed much in establishing the Madawaska Training School. Dickey Hall was constructed in 1914 and served as a dormitory and dining facility. The building on the right is the old Cyr Hall. The building on the left was Nowland Hall. Dickey Hall was demolished in 1969.

In 1906, the Catholic church in Fort Kent, under the leadership of Fr. Arthur Decary, was successful in acquiring the services of the Little Franciscans of Mary to staff what became known as St. Louis School. Enrollment grew to a point where there were concerns with overcrowded conditions. This school, from 1911 to 1929, also operated as a boarding school. In the early years, the sisters provided instruction through the high school years. Because of pressing enrollment demands, a new St. Louis School building with 25 classrooms was built in 1922. This photograph dates to the 1930s.

Stephen Audibert was a successful businessman as well as a devout Catholic. His twin daughters were educated at the convent school and later joined the congregation of Little Franciscan Sisters. Both had successful teaching careers, spending a total of 59 years teaching at St. Louis School. From left to right here are Irene, who was known in religion as Sister Mary Etienne-du-Sacré Coeur, and Margaerite who was Sister Marie-Arthur-de-Jésus.

In 1920, the town built a high school facility on what is now the front lawn of Community High School. Some students could "bypass" the high school and enroll in a teacher-training program at Madawaska Training School, which included an accelerated secondary program. When surrounding towns joined Fort Kent in a consolidation effort, the high school quickly became overcrowded. That required double sessions and the building of what is now known as the "freshmen wing" of the high school complex. In 1957, the main building of the high school was completed, and the old structure was torn down. In 1968, a new addition was added consisting of a library, cafeteria, and music and driver's education rooms.

In 1943, two-thirds of the students in Fort Kent attended St. Louis School; the other third were scattered in 11 rural school buildings under the direction of 14 teachers. The high enrollment at St. Louis School moved the town to build a new school, called Market Street School, in 1951. The school committee asked the Little Franciscan Sisters to staff the new facility. When Market Street School opened, the pupil load at St. Louis School was reduced from over 900 to less than 700.

In the early years, Fort Kent High School offered a course in agriculture. This is a 1948 photograph of the Future Farmers of America club at the high school. Seen here are, from left to right, (first row) Roland Daigle, Jack Bouchard, teacher Alton Bridges, Thomas Clavette, and Carl Pinette; (second row) Bernard Nadeau, Reynold Pelletier, Gilbert Lozier, Edmund Bouchard, and Norman Desjardin; (third row) ? Pelletier, Elroy Daigle, Paul Desjardin, Donald Daigle, Howard Paradis, and Louis Morin.

A sister that is particularly well remembered was Soeur Marie-Jean-du-Cénacle, known to students as Mother John. She was a Massachusetts native who spent 31 years in Fort Kent, six of those years as superior and nine years as school principal. She completed a graduate degree in English at Laval University in Quebec and was well respected for her skills as teacher and administrator. In 1998, she died at the age of 96 at the infirmary of the congregation in Baie-Saint-Paul, Quebec.

In the fall of 1965, a group of Fort Kent citizens organized to create a new institution of higher learning. This effort developed into John F. Kennedy College, a private, non-profit four-year institution. The college was situated on the south side of East Main Street. The prime mover of the college was its president, Claude Charette. In 1969, the school had an enrollment of 87 full- and part-time students with 21 mostly adjunct faculty. While the effort was noble, John F. Kennedy College faced particularly challenging times with recruitment and finance. It eventually closed.

Four

Fort Kent's Unending Natural Disasters

Over the years, the many floods that plagued Fort Kent created hardship and devastation. The photograph shows water inundation on West Main Street in the spring of 1933. It was understandable that the settlers wanted to be close to the rivers for transportation. However, these low-lying areas abutting the rivers were susceptible to flooding.

In 1933, the spring flooding, according to some older members of the community, proved to be one of the most disastrous moments of history for Fort Kent. Newspaper reports carried the following story on the 1933 flood: "More than 200 families have been forced from their homes and thousands of dollars worth of property damage has been caused by the St. John River. Fort Kent alone estimates $15,000 worth of property damage. It was a busy week for Fort Kent storekeepers in salvaging their property from cellars and even first floors. It proved a help for the unemployed as more than a hundred received work."

This early 20th century photograph is of the spring flooding of West Main Street. Significant flooding was reported in the years 1958, 1961, 1968, 1969, 1970, and 1973. In May 1961, water levels rose to 26.58 feet. Water was reported to be one to two feet deep along the length of Main Street. A resident reported anxiously "watching the water creep into his cellar, flood it, and then start on the backyard. I couldn't do a thing about it." In 1979, the St. John River crested at a record height and, once again, overflowed its banks. The St. John crested at 27.3 feet. In homes, furniture was raised and belongings were piles on beds. Appliances were moved in an attempt to place them out of water's reach. According to the town's civil defense director, water had never before settled in the St. Louis Catholic Church parking lot as it did that year. The two-year-old earthen dike, however, saved the downtown business district from flooding. The flood was attributed to rain coinciding with warm weather. The 1979 flood damaged to residential area of Fort Kent was estimated at $500,000. To protect West Main Street, a dike was constructed in 1977.

Again in the spring of 2008, the St. John and Fish Rivers reaches record levels, causing extreme flooding. Roads were closed, as was the international and Fish River bridges. It also caused the evacuation of over 600 people. Flooding was caused by a heavy snowfall combined with at least three inches of rain and snowmelt. Officials ordered a mandatory evacuation of some downtown areas, forcing business owners who were emptying their stores of merchandise to leave. As Fish River overran its western bank near where it joins the St. John River, water began flowing into the business district, taking an unobstructed route behind the dike that protects West Main Street from the St. John River. The municipal public works crew, along with local volunteers helped create a berm to stem the flow, allowing several pumps to keep up with the water seeping through. The St. John River rose 8.1 feet in less than 24 hours and surged over 30 feet, well over above the 25-foot flood stage. Flood damage sustained by St. Louis Catholic Church exceeded $1 million. In the West Main Street area, the water got dangerously close to the top of the levee. Scientists described the flooding for the community as "greater than a 100-year event." The photograph shows the high waters that almost overcame the International Bridge and levee on West Main Street.

Five

AMONG CIVIC-MINDED CITIZENS

Inseparably linked with the history of Fort Kent is the career of Maj. William Dickey, who was dearly referred to as the father of the Madawaska territory. Throughout the state of Maine, he was also known as "a protector of the French race." When he died at the age of 90 in 1899, Dickey had served a total of 33 terms on the Maine legislature. Dickey once remarked that in Fort Kent, "there is no more beautiful country you can find." He particularly liked Fort Kent's sunset view. "There is no place this side of London where you can see such beautiful scenery as in that sunset."

This 1890s photograph shows Maj. William Dickey with one of his grandsons. During his extended legislative career, Dickey was proud of his labors "in the interest and for the welfare of the Acadian people." It was said that he became for the region their good St. Nicolas, for he always returned from the legislature "laden with wonderful tokens for the stockings of a pleased and faithful constituency!" The last time he appeared in the legislature was in 1897 at the age of 88 years. Dickey often jocosely remarked that in an earlier time he wondered about and, in seeking a healthier place, found Fort Kent. Most of all, Dickey was held in very high esteem by his constituents.

Cyrus Henry Dickey was the youngest son of Maj. William Dickey who remained in the area and established himself in the lumbering business. Until 1895, Cyrus lived in Frenchville, where he was partnered with Eaton in lumbering. He later moved to Fort Kent and went in business on his own in buying and shipping shingles. It was Cyrus who cared for his father during the last years of his life. Cyrus married Leanna Mallett on January 10, 1899, and they had no children. The community was saddened to learn that Cyrus took his own life on September 8, 1927 when he was 77 years of age.

William married Lydia Frances Bodfish of Gardner in 1842, the same year that the state of Maine granted him 2,000 acres for a gristmill in Fort Kent. Lydia was a fond and devoted partner to her husband. At the age of 52, Lydia died of typhoid fever in Fort Kent. Her obituary described her as a woman of strong Christian faith. The Dickey family consisted of three sons and two daughters. William became a captain in the Civil War and eventually settled in Louisiana. Calvin Dickey eventually settled in the West and also distinguished himself in the Civil War. Cyrus remained in Fort Kent and carried on an extensive trade in lumber. It was he who took care of his father in his last years. Margaret married a prominent local lawyer and general businessman, G. A. Fenlason, and Cora married Willie Cunliffe, a lumberman.

The Dickey Residence, Fort Kent, Me.

Cyrus Henry Dickey's home was an early landmark that was situated on the bank of the Fish River, directly opposite the Hotel Dickey. It was thought to have been used for solders' quarters during the Aroostook War. The property was later owned by Dr. Richard Savage and Harold Daigle. The area occupied by the house was considered as the location for the proposed hospital in the early 1950s. The idea was rejected because the lot was too small. The building was subsequently torn down.

Margaret, Major Dickey's oldest daughter, attended the Madawaska Training School and later married A. G. Fenlason, a prominent local lawyer. Margaret had a lifelong interest in the history of Fort Kent, being often referred to as the historian of Colonial Fort Kent.

Dr. Rosario Jean-Baptiste Page's home in Fort Kent, seen in this photograph taken in 1920, was situated where Lawrence Workman's house is currently located in West Main Street. The house burned in 1925 when son Simon Page left a hot iron on the ironing board and went to join the family at a horse race in Clair, New Brunswick. After the loss of their home, the family then lived in the house seen in background that was originally owned by the Bradburys.

Major Dickey's youngest daughter was Dora, who married William Cunliffe Jr., a well-known lumberman in the area. William represented the second generation of lumber operators in the region. He was the son of William H. Cunliffe Sr., a New Brunswick native who entered the employ of Shepard Cary of Houlton and was sent to Fort Kent to manage the interests of the Cary lumber enterprise.

A particularly well-liked early doctor was Dr. Richard Savage. Much of his time was spent going from one end of the territory to the other delivering babies. It was not uncommon to deliver a dozen babies within a 24-hour period. He was born in Fort Kent in 1899. His father was William Savage, a store owner and mailman. His mother was Edith Daigle Savage, a schoolteacher. Dr. Savage graduated from the University of Montreal Medical School in 1925 and settled in Fort Kent to practice his profession. Shown in this 1954 photograph are the medical staff at Peoples' Benevolent Hospital. They are, from left to right, (first row) Dr. Richard Savage, Dr. Melvin Aungst, Dr. Leonide Toussaint, and Dr. Leonce Albert; (second row) Dr. Thomas Levesque, Dr. Fernand Normand, Dr. Maurice Cyr, Dr. Fernand Normandeau, and Dr. D. Albert, radiologist.

Dr. Leonce Albert, M.D., was a Fort Kent medical doctor that served the area people with a great deal of zeal and compassion. He attended school at Saint-Anne-de-la-Pocatiere in Quebec and graduated in 1925 from the medical school at Laval University. Dr. Albert resided most of his life in Fort Kent. For 25 years, he was a member and the examining physician for the Catholic Order of Foresters. He also served as a medical examiner for selective service during World War II. When a hospital was established in town, he was among the first to be on the medical staff.

This 2006 photograph is of, from left to right, Randall Pinkham, George Pooler, and Bill Pinkham on a fishing excursion in Alaska. Randall is a graduate of the local high school and the University of Maine in Orono. He was in the navy for three years and worked for Bill until his retirement. Randall spent many years in public service that included chairing the town council, being on the library committee, and serving on the planning board. He was recognized for his community service by being named Fort Kent's outstanding citizen by the chamber of commerce. The Pinkhams are descendents of a pioneering family of Fort Kent. Bill continued in the family business of lumbering and his enterprise provided employment for many in the area.

Paul D. Thibodeau moved to Fort Kent in 1904 and in 1906 married Mary Alice Nadeau, the granddaughter of the first settler of Fort Kent. He then started his own insurance business, calling it the Thibodeau Insurance Agency. Selling being a skill of his, Paul also became the distributor for Maxwell Automobiles throughout the valley and on to Fort Fairfield, Portage, Ashland, Stockholm, and New Sweden. When the First National Bank opened its doors in Fort Kent in 1911, Paul became one of the bank's directors and later president of the only valley bank that did not cease operation during the Great Depression years. Ever interested in his community, Paul served as town treasurer in 1913, was elected to the legislature in 1915, and became president of the Fort Kent Historical Society. He authored a pamphlet on the early history of Fort Kent, which the bank published. Two of his children entered religious life. Ludger became a Franciscan priest and was for a time president of St. Francis College in Biddeford, Maine. Juliette, known as Sister Mary Paulina, was a sister of Mercy in Portland.

James Hoyt, pictured in this photograph of the 1940s, established a distinguished record of community service. He was a charter member and held all offices of the Fort Kent Lion's Club. He was also an organizer of the Fort Kent Volunteer Fire Department and served as member for 30 years. Hoyt was chairman of the Fort Kent Red Cross Chapter from 1943 until his death in 1984. He was director of the Fort Kent Playground Association and was the Fort Kent Golf Club's first manager.

For many years, when the people in Fort Kent heard the name "Soucy," they thought of business. Alfred D. Soucy was the son of Denis and Dorumene Pelletier Soucy. He attended Fort Kent schools and graduated from the Madawaska Training School. After leaving the service at the end of World War I, he went into the grocery business here for some 56 years. In 1937, he was acknowledged as the first to open a self-service, independently-owned grocery store in the eastern United States. He was a member of the American Legion in Fort Kent and was instrumental in the construction of Fort Kent's first American Legion Post home. Soucy was also a fourth degree member of the Knights of Columbus and past president of the Rotary Club, and a member of the Senior Citizen Housing Committee and the Fort Kent Housing Committee. Soucy was a member the committee responsible for bringing a hospital in Fort Kent and served as the first president of the board of trustees in 1952. He remained a member of the board until his death in 1974.

This photograph shows the grocery store owned by Soucy. He belonged to several professional associations of grocers and served as a director of the Maine Retail Grocers Association.

The homestead of the Soucy family is on East Main Street. The photograph was taken around 1905 with the family standing in front of the house. On the porch are Alfred's parents, Denis and Dorumene Pelletier Soucy. Standing between his parents was Alfred. The house is currently the home of Lise and David Soucy.

Alphee J. Nadeau contributed significantly to Fort Kent's community life and development. He was the founder of the A. J. Nadeau and Sons Hardware and Sporting Goods store. He also owned the Nadeau Funeral Home. Nadeau was married in 1908 to Delvina (Plourde) Nadeau of St. Jacque, New Brunswick. The union brought forth 10 children. He retired in 1951. This 1950s photograph is of Alphee and Delvina.

David D. Daigle was a well-known area farmer as well as a prominent civic and business leader in the community. Besides his farming interests, he owned the Daigle and Daigle Furniture and Hardware Store, and a funeral business in town. Daigle served on the board of Maine Public Service Company, Northern National Bank, and the Bangor and Aroostook Railroad Company. In this 1918 picture are, from left to right, David Daigle holding three-year-old John, 13-year-old James, and wife Irene holding one-year-old Janet May. Absent for the photograph was 15-year-old Peggy.

Dr. Irenee Cyr spent a lifetime serving the area as a dentist and had two sons who also became dentists. Cyr graduated from the Madawaska Training School in 1912 and was enrolled at the Baltimore College of Dental Surgery, where he graduated with a doctor of dental surgery degree on 1918. Cyr served his country during World War I and was a charter member and post commander of the American Legion Martin-Klein Post No. 133. He was a member of the local selective service board, a director of Peoples' Benevolent Hospital in Fort Kent, and a member of the medical dental staff of the hospital. Dr. Cyr was home service director of the Fort Kent Chapter of the American Red Cross.

Harry L. Etscovitz was a prominent local businessman who, over the years, contributed substantially to Fort Kent's improvements and economic development. Etscovitz attended Fort Kent High School in 1938 and went on graduate from Harvard University in 1942. Since college graduation, Etscovitz was in business in Fort Kent. With his farming and car dealer enterprises, Etscovitz employed many people. His community involvement included being a director of the local chamber of commerce, trustee of the public library, and on the Board of Peoples' Benevolent Hospital. He was a member of the Martin-Klein Post of the American Legion, and a member of the Masonic lodge and the Lions Club. In 1972, the Fort Kent Chamber of Commerce recognized him for his business and community accomplishments by naming him the "Outstanding Citizen of the Year." This is a 1940s photograph of his business.

The Paradis family in Fort Kent has been in the grocery business since the 1930s. Later the patriarch of the family Louis J. and his sons Leo, Quentin, and Roger started the business in the Roy building on the corner of Market and Main Streets. The business was small at first but expansions in 1960 and 1964 made use of every available space in the building. As the business kept growing, a move to new quarters at the corner of Pleasant and Main Streets became necessary. Over the years, the business had various affiliations such as Nationwide, IGA, and Shop and Save. Since the start of the business, different Paradis men and women have entered the firm, as it was a large family of 11 boys and 5 girls. Louis was a member of the Fort Kent Rotary Club, Knights of Columbus, and the Catholic Order of Foresters. This prominent Fort Kent businessman died in 1968 at the age of 75. Louis J. was born in Fort Kent, May 3, 1893, the son of George and Flavie (Long) Paradis. The 1950s photograph is of Louis in front of his store in the P. V. Roy building.

Irenee Cyr was an outstanding citizen of Fort Kent. A staunch democrat throughout life, he represented Fort Kent in the state legislature in 1911, 1913, 1949, 1953, and 1955. In between times, he was named postmaster in Fort Kent, where he served for seven years. In 1920, Cyr helped organize the First National Bank of Fort Kent, and he was its first cashier. He was proud that, and with the help of colleagues he was able to bring the registry of deed's office to Fort Kent. He was also proud of his efforts to "upgrade" the local college to Fort Kent State Teachers' College. He was also particularly proud of his family that included three lawyers, two postmasters, a nurse, and a public accountant. Cyr was prominent in the civic affairs of the town, serving as chairman of the school board for many years, and trustee of Community High School District No. 1, the first of its kind in the state. He was married to the late Elodie Pinette. In later years, he remarried to Phoebe (Boutot) Cyr.

Six

THE FAITH THAT SUSTAINED MANY

This early 1900 panoramic view is of the Catholic church complex in Fort Kent. To the right is the church that was destroyed by fire on March 30, 1907. On the left is the church rectory that housed the priest. The small center building that served as the first convent was commonly referred to the *presbytère des habitants*. It was so called because during inclement weather, the building was used to shelter parishioners as they waited for church services to begin. While Fort Kent was a home for Catholics for some time, it was years without a church. For church services, it was customary for the early settlers to paddle in canoes to Saint-Basile in New Brunswick and later to St. Luce in Frenchville for church services.

It was in 1875 that Fort Kent received its first resident pastor, Fr. Cleophas Demers. In addition to ministering in Fort Kent, Father Demers also was assigned mission churches in St. Francis and Wallagrass. On an annual basis, he made pastoral visits to minister to lumberman employed in wood camps from Ashland to the areas of Little Black River and the Castonguay farm. After seven years of service, Demers asked to be relieved of his post for health reasons. He was then assigned to a parish in Somersworth, New Hampshire, where he remained until his death in 1906.

During his last years in Fort Kent, Father Demers initiated the construction of a new bigger church to replace the chapel that could no longer accommodate the growing Catholic population. This church, measuring 90 feet by 45 feet, was built where the former convent building, now an apartment complex, stood. The old chapel sacristy, measuring 30 by 20 feet, was attached to the new church. Although far from finished, mass was celebrated in the new church on Sunday, September 3, 1882.

The interior of the church was ornate as was common of early Catholic churches. The sanctuary contained a main altar and two side altars. A communion rail separated the vestibule from the church proper.

In 1884, plans were drawn to build the rectory but the actual construction began only in 1886. It was first occupied on October 25, 1886. Between 1919 and 1925, additions to the rear of the rectory were made to provide quarters for the housekeeper. The rectory was situated in the vicinity of the current funeral home on East Main Street.

The French settlers that settled in Fort Kent were devout Catholics who often expressed their faith publicly by celebrating religious feast days in a public fashion. One of the feasts celebrated was Fete-Dieu, otherwise known as the feast of Corpus Christi, which was celebrated on Thursday following Trinity Sunday, usually occurring in May or June. The Blessed Sacrament was carried by the parish priest, holding high in triumph a monstrance with the Holy Eucharist. It recalled the Lord's prophecy "The Son of Man must be lifted up" (John 3:14). The devotion usually started with mass, exposition, and the Litany of the Saints. The procession about town recalled God's presence with humanity in its earthy journey. It also provided opportunity for public adoration and a means to sanctify and bless the people, streets, and homes by the presence of Jesus Christ. A canopy, held over the priest, was carried by four ushers that were usually members of the parish. The procession was lead by acolytes carrying the processional cross, flanked with candle holders. The early 1920s photograph shows the adoration procession at the Michaud house on Pleasant Street.

Fort Kent's second pastor was Fr. Francois-Xavier Burque, who remained in Fort Kent until 1904. The partially-completed new church was finished under the direction of Father Burque. Burque was a much-loved man and a dear friend and supporter of Maj. William Dickey. When Burque from the pulpit urged his parishioners to support Dickey in an election, the bishop was not pleased. As a result, Father Burque was reassigned elsewhere in 1896. A petition was circulated by Amaziah G. Fenlason (Dickey's brother-in-law) to have Burque remain in Fort Kent. The petition was presented to the bishop who reversed his decision and allowed Burque to remain in Fort Kent for eight more years, until he retired in 1904. Following Major Dickey's death, Burque wrote an eloquent biography of him.

Fr. Arthur Decary was Fort Kent's third pastor, arriving here in 1904 and remaining until 1919. Decary was successful in acquiring the services of the Little Franciscan Sisters of Mary that staffed a school and later the hospital in Fort Kent. During his tenure, a fire destroyed the church on March 30, 1907. The fire likely originated in the cellar near the furnace.

The Fort Kent mission of the Little Franciscans of Mary was initially staffed in 1906 by the following four sisters, seen here. Seated from left to right are Sister Marie-Gertrude and Sister Marie l'Ange Guardien; standing from left to right are Sister Marie-Candide and Sister Marie-Antoine-de-Padoue, superior. Upon arrival, the sisters were disappointed in the lack of instructional materials and primitive quarters. The sisters opened two classes on September 10, 1906, with 106 pupils. The third class was opened the following month, and a fourth one on January 20, 1907. Their faith sustained them, and they remained in Fort Kent to provide services.

Delina Daigle, a Fort Kent native, was one of the first from the area to enter religious life. Daigle attended the Madawaska Training School to complete the teacher-training program. For about 12 years, she taught in area rural schools. She felt called to be a teaching nun and entered the convent in 1904, at 28 years of age. Delina became know in religion as Sister Candide, and she enjoyed a successful teaching career with 28 of those years in Fort Kent.

In 1909, the foundation was laid for the current church. The exterior brickwork was completed by December 1910, and the first mass was celebrated in this church on January 15, 1911. However, the interior was not fully completed until 1914. The photograph shows an architectural rendition of what the church was to be. A spire to cap the tower was not completed as planned. Engineers did not feel that the foundation was adequate to hold its weight.

Before building a new church, the parish quickly engaged in constructing a building that would have a dual purpose. The first floor of the building would provide classrooms and an apartment for the sisters. It was ready for occupancy in December 1907. The second story was used to celebrate mass until the new church would be built. The parish census in 1908 reflected "550 families" with 2,850 souls. Some 250 students, including some that were not Catholic, attended the school in 1907.

This photograph, dated 1911, shows the new church when its exterior was completed.

Fr. Raoul Bourbeau replaced Fr. Arthur Decary in 1919 and remained in Fort Kent six years. An overcrowded school facility was the pressing concern during his tenure as pastor. During the 1921–1922 school year, there were 24 Little Franciscan Sisters teaching 661 pupils.

Father Joseph A. Normand was Fort Kent's fifth Catholic pastor, arriving here in 1925 and remaining until 1934. He is remembered in the parish as a "deeply religious and spiritual" man. Some were convinced that he had healing powers.

ECOLE ST. LOUIS, FORT KENT, ME. 10K.

Work on St. Louis School, now an apartment complex, was begun on July 9, 1923. A corner stone blessing was held on September 2, 1923. The school was ready for occupancy for the 1924–1925 school year. The school was a quasi Catholic-public school in that the town paid the teachers and helped with heating cost. Each member of the religious staff was simply given a small stipend, approximately half of what lay teachers earned. The school was closed in 1969 when the Fort Kent Elementary School was opened.

Succeeding Fr. Joseph Normand as the sixth pastor in Fort Kent was Fr. Aime Giguere, who arrived in St. Louis in 1834 and remained until 1951, some 17 years. Father Giguere organized an effort to establish a hospital in Fort Kent. Local fund drives raised a total of $114,000 for the hospital. A movie theater was also established in the basement of the convent that raised $60,000 for the project. The remaining funds needed for the hospital came from a federal grant and the Little Franciscan Sisters who were asked to staff it.

It was always a joy for parishioners when the bishop of the diocese visited to administer the sacrament of confirmation. In the 1960s, Bishop Daniel Feeney is shown in procession as he leaves the church for the rectory. The children receiving the sacrament are shown here lined up along the path, with the girls on one side and the boys on the other. For the occasion, boys dressed in a suit and girls wore a white dress and veil, symbolizing the white garment of baptism. (Courtesy of Connie Michaud.)

The eighth pastor, Fr. Wilfrid Soucy, was the first native son to be pastor of St. Louis. He came here in 1962 and remained here some five years. During his tenure, Soucy built a new rectory and initiated church renovations according to Vatican II guidelines. A long-awaited church steeple made of lightweight aluminum material was installed in 1963. Soucy is remembered in the community as a priest who "got things done" and one who "dared" in the face of challenges. He always remembered his years in Fort Kent as the "highlight" of his career.

Fr. Adrien H. Palardy had the distinction of being the seventh pastor, arriving here in 1951 and leaving in 1962, a period of 11 years. With considerable festivity, the parish community of Fort Kent celebrated Palardy's 25th anniversary to the priesthood in 1954. Concerts were organized under the direction of the sisters for the event. Palardy was considered a very devoted pastor who had a commanding presence and was not easily challenged. Palardy undertook the project of getting local families to sponsor new stained-glass windows in the church. The stained-glass windows, designed by Fraz Schroeder from Librairie St-Michel in Boston, were added in 1956.

PRESBYTERIAN CHURCH, FT. KENT. ME. 13

During the end of the 19th century, the Protestant community in Fort Kent organized for the purpose of building a church. On June 6, 1895, a meeting of the Protestant community was held at the office of A. J. Fenlason with Rev. James Ross acting as chairman. W. H. Cunliffe, treasurer, reported the sum of $511.73 on hand. The following individuals were appointed as trustees: G. V. Cunliffe, A. J. Fenlason, B. W. Mallett, A. M. Pinkham, and Thomas Bradbury. The following were appointed to the building committee: W. H. Cunliffe, Cyrus Dickey, and Lester F. Bradbury. They were directed to look after a site for the church and report to the congregation within one week.

The committee's work was quickly completed. Construction of the church was begun in the latter part of 1895 and completed in 1896. The church bell, which weighs 1,200 pounds, was bought and installed the following year. The church remained Presbyterian until the United Church of Canada came into being. The congregation then voted to join with the Congregational Church of Maine.

Seven

PICTURESQUE FORT KENT

Fort Kent was described as being surrounded by "a great and fertile farming country" that developed into the shipping point of the area's timber and farm products. It became an important trading center in northern Maine. The region was depicted as being very hilly with numerous waterways and lush vegetation that made the area one of the most attractive on the eastern North American continent. Early amateur and professional photographers were drawn to its scenic beauty. The photographs, dated in the early to late 20th century, depict the town's scenic panoramic views and architectural beauties. In this distant view of the village, there are some easily identified early landmarks such as the Madawaska Training School and the old Catholic church.

This is an early view of the Fish River taken from the St. John River. Seen are Pleasant Street buildings, including the Madawaska Training School.

This picture shows a panoramic view of Fort Kent taken from the Canadian side of the St. John River. The setting for the town was naturally picturesque. Lofty hills rose at a distance from the river banks while near the water the land "lied in gradually receding terraces of fertile soil," according to Edward Wiggin.

FISH RIVER FT. KENT ME.

In this panoramic view of Fort Kent is seen the Madawaska Training School at the center of the photograph. The picture was taken from the Fish River, looking at the school buildings on Pleasant Street.

This photograph is also a panoramic view of Fort Kent. It is a view of Pleasant Street, taken from the bank of the Fish River.

This view of Fort Kent was taken from the vicinity of what is now St. Louis Church cemetery, near the medical center. It was originally printed in the *Industrial Journal* of Bangor in 1908.

This early postcard views Fort Kent from the riverside. Pictured is the St. John River and the International Bridge connecting Fort Kent to Clair, New Brunswick.

The picture is of Fort Kent, taken from the Klein Hill area of town, and shows an overview of the village. The St. John River cuts across the center of the photograph. The view is of West Main Street with a premature Hall Street.

This photograph looks at Hall Street and the West Main Street area.

FISH RIVER, FORT KENT MAINE   1939

These pictures show views of the Fish River. Edward Wiggin, an early writer, described the Fish River as "flowing southward through a magnificent chain of lakes and becoming a noble river before it poured its volume into the St. John."

FISH RIVER NEAR FORT KENT

BIBLIOGRAPHY

Baker, Van R. (ed.) *Webster: Letters of an Army Family in Peace and War, 1836–1853*. Kent, OH: Kent State University Press, 2000.

Blakey, Arch Fredric. *General John H. Winder*. Gainesville: University of Florida Press, 1990.

Byrne and Leahy. *History of the Catholic Church: The New England States*. Boston: the Hurd and Everts Company, 1899.

Daigle, Laurel J. *Fort Kent's St. Louis Church 1870–1995*. 1996.

Fort Kent Centennial Book. Madawaska, ME: St. John Valley Publishing, 1969.

Fort Kent Railroad Station Brochure. Fort Kent Historical Society, 1985.

Industrial Journal. Bangor, ME: 1906.

Wiggin, Edward. *History of Aroostook County, Maine*. Presque Isle, ME: the Star Herald Press, 1922.

ACROSS AMERICA, PEOPLE ARE DISCOVERING SOMETHING WONDERFUL. *THEIR HERITAGE.*

Arcadia Publishing is the leading local history publisher in the United States. With more than 3,000 titles in print and hundreds of new titles released every year, Arcadia has extensive specialized experience chronicling the history of communities and celebrating America's hidden stories, bringing to life the people, places, and events from the past. To discover the history of other communities across the nation, please visit:

www.arcadiapublishing.com

Customized search tools allow you to find regional history books about the town where you grew up, the cities where your friends and family live, the town where your parents met, or even that retirement spot you've been dreaming about.

CPSIA information can be obtained
at www.ICGtesting.com
Printed in the USA
LVHW060918160621
690369LV00003B/121